PAGASQUEENY'S PANTRY

- -

A short play for middle or high school

by
Jackie Jernigan

plus . . . . *four student monologues/duets*

www.studentplays.org
john@studentplays.org

<u>Copyright information. Please read!</u>

☞ **About Student Plays** ☜

Student Plays consists of **John Glass, Jackie Jernigan,** and **Dominic Torres**. We are a group of playwrights and directors that have written scripts for middle school, high school, and the university. We are proud of the variety of ages that our scripts serve, and we are particularly proud of our *Latino-themed plays*. These are scripts that focus on Latino youths and the Latino experience. Any school can perform a Latino-themed play: it just requires a general introduction and exposure to the Spanish language, something that most schools and students already have.

To learn more, or to communicate with one of the playwrights, contact us at john@studentplays.org.

PAGASQUEENY'S PANTRY

Characters

PHOEBE: Female. Bossy. Works for Pagasqueeny.

BO: A follower. Goofy.

LINDA: Nice, responsible. Aware of doing the right thing.

PAGASQUEENY: Elderly Italian-American man. Could be played by student with wig and proper clothing, or a teacher.

JESSIE: Grandchild of Pagasqueeny. Minor role. 6 - 10 years old. Any gender.

LUKE: Grandchild of Pagasqueeny. Minor role. 6-10 years old. Any gender.

The time is the present, the setting a kitchen and pantry in Mr. Pagasqueeny's house. Any kind of table or tables can be used, and there should be a large amount of typical kitchen clutter on the tables.

PHOEBE, BO, and LINDA are all hiding in a pantry, talking as they secretly watch Pagasqueeny. The pantry can be a simple construction of cardboard, or even a long table on its end. Anything simple could be used to portray a pantry wall between the actors and Mr. Pagasqueeny.

** The characters of JESSIE and LUKE are meant to be younger than the other students but any student can perform these two roles. **

As the lights go up, BO, LINDA, and PHOEBE have just snuck into the kitchen. They hurriedly look through the items on the table.

PHOEBE: Gotta be in here somewhere.

BO: Pagasqueeny has clutter!

LINDA: Sheesh. *(Picking up something.)* No kidding.

PHOEBE: Put that down, Linda!

LINDA: What? I'm just looking.

PHOEBE: You're supposed to be looking for my money!

BO: What color is it, Phoebe?

PHOEBE: Blue. It was in a blue envelope.

LINDA: I didn't know you worked for a hoarder!

BO: I know. Wow.

LINDA: *(Picking up baton.)* Look at this! Is this Pagasqueeny's conducting baton?

PHOEBE: Linda!

LINDA: What? I'm only—

(She knocks a cup of pencils over, spilling everywhere.)

PHOEBE: Look at what you did!

LINDA: Relax! We'll just clean it up.

BO: Come on, hurry.

(They all stoop down to pick the pencils up.)

PHOEBE: I can't believe you.

LINDA: They're only pencils, Phoebe.

PHOEBE: I knew I shouldn't have brought you in here.

BO: Phoebe! What was that noise???

PHOEBE: What?

LINDA: I didn't hear anything!

BO: Listen!

(A noise at the door is heard.)

PHOEBE: It's Pagasqueeny. He's here!

BO: Oh no!

PHOEBE: Come on!

(They quickly stand up.)

LINDA: What do we do?

BO: I don't want to go to jail!

PHOEBE: Come on, let's hide in here!

LINDA: Where?

PHOEBE: Be quiet and follow me! Hurry!

> *(They scramble into the pantry. Pause. In walks PAGASQUEENY. He puts a newspaper and keys down on the table, begins to prepare a meal. PHOEBE walks right to the peephole and watches him.)*

PHOEBE: I can't believe this!

BO: This little room is cool!

PHOEBE: What's he doing here!

LINDA: *(Noticing the hole.)* Phoebe, what is that?

PHOEBE: It's a little hole that I cut in the pantry wall. Sometimes I come in here and eat a snack and relax.

BO: You *what*??

PHOEBE: Sometimes when I'm working I come in here and just chill. You know. I made this little hole where I can watch him in case he comes in the kitchen.

LINDA: You're crazy!

BO: That's so cool! I want to see!

PHOEBE: Quiet!! *(Pause. She motions BO to take a look.)* Here, take a look. I can't believe Pagasqueeny is here! He's supposed to be out of town, at some dumb music conference.

BO: This is sweet! We can spy on him!

PHOEBE: Not so loud!

LINDA: I thought you said he was deaf!

PHOEBE: Well, he is. But still, keep your voices down.

BO: Okay. Phoebe, what are we going to do?

PHOEBE: I don't know! Linda, this is all your fault.

LINDA: How??

PHOEBE: You knocked those pencils over! We could have found my money and left! But *you* made a mess!

LINDA: He's old. He'll never see it.

PAGASQUEENY: *(Discovering mess.)* What IS this?? That girl is so messy!

BO: Actually, I think he just found out.

PHOEBE: Ohh!!! See? He *does* know.

PAGASQUEENY: And where are my donuts??

BO: I think he wants his donuts.

PHOEBE: Oh. Yeah, I think I may have eaten those.

PAGASQUEENY: That girl misplaces everything.

LINDA: Look. He'll leave pretty soon and we'll just go, right? What's the big deal?

PHOEBE: The big deal is that I shouldn't have brought *you* in here. I should have just brought Bo.

LINDA: You asked *both* of us to come with you!! You said you were scared to come into this house alone!!

PHOEBE: Oh, whatever. I was just saying that.

LINDA: Here, let me have a look.

(Pause as she moves in take a peek beside BO.)

PHOEBE: What's he doing, Bo?

BO: Looking for something. Probably still wants his donuts.

PAGASQUEENY: Where *are* those donuts??

BO: Yep. He wants his donuts.

PHOEBE: Silly old man. He can buy those anytime.

LINDA: Phoebe, what's he like?

PHOEBE: Mr. Pagasqueeny? I told you guys. He's annoying. Just because he's a high school orchestra conductor he thinks he's the world's *best* conductor. He always playing that loud music in the house. Always wants *horseradish* on his food. Tells me to return things *where they belong.*

BO: Really?

PHOEBE: Really. He's horrible. We haven't been getting along lately.

LINDA: Well, at least you have a job.

PHOEBE: Huh?

LINDA: Seriously. This seems like a pretty cool job.

BO: Yeah. You don't have to wear a uniform or anything.

PHOEBE: You guys have no idea. Pagasqueeny's bossy.

LINDA: But at least you are making some money! I can't find a part-time job anywhere.

PAGASQUEENY: Where are my napkins??

BO: And you get paid in cash!

PHOEBE: It doesn't matter. He's annoying. And speaking of cash, do you guys see the envelope?? Look for it.

LINDA: I still don't see it.

BO: Wait. There's something there. Way over there on the small table.

LINDA: Yep. That might be it, Phoebe. It's by those magazines.

PHOEBE: Let me see. *(She looks.)*

BO: On the small table. At the very back. See it?

PHOEBE: That's it!!

PAGASQUEENY: Where is my wheat bread??

PHOEBE: *(Groaning.)* Agghh! The bread!

BO: What?

PHOEBE: He wants wheat bread! I was supposed to get some yesterday and I didn't.

PAGASQUEENY: That girl . . . !

PHOEBE: Oh, this is terrible. My life is over. I just want to get my money and get out of here!!

BO: Well, come on, Phoebe. At least you got paid your normal check.

LINDA: Huh?

PHOEBE: It doesn't matter. I want that money.

LINDA: He already paid you?

PHOEBE: Yes, if you *must* know. It's his fault if he wants to pay me twice in the same week.

BO: That's right!

LINDA: So . . . he's already paid you? And he forgot?

PHOEBE: Yes. His loss, my gain.

LINDA: Phoebe . . . do you really feel that way?

PHOEBE: Well, actually, yes. I do. Come on. He's old and forgetful.

LINDA: You should return that money.

PHOEBE: I told you, it's his fault if he wants to pay me twice.

BO: Yeah! He's rich, right? He'll never know that he overpaid you.

PHOEBE: That's exactly right.

LINDA: Wow.

PHOEBE: And just who are you? Mother Teresa?

LINDA: No, but--

PHOEBE: But what?

LINDA: That's just not honest. I didn't know that he already paid you.

PHOEBE: *(With scorn.)* Mind your own business!

BO: Yeah!

LINDA: *(Hurt.)* Okay. Sorry.

PHOEBE: This is *my* problem, not yours.

LINDA: I'll be quiet.

PHOEBE: Now, come on, enough of all this. We gotta come up with something. *(She looks through the hole.)* I don't know why I put it by those magazines. I had to work yesterday and I must have put it down before I left. *(Pops herself across the forehead.)* Ridiculous!

BO: We'll just have to wait it out, Phoebe.

PHOEBE: Ughhh.

> *(LINDA notices a hanging chef's hat or apron and quickly puts it on, and then begins to mime somebody.)*

LINDA: Hey guys, look. Who am I?

BO: What are you doing?

LINDA: Guess who I am!

PHOEBE: We aren't in the mood for games. Tell us.

LINDA: I'm Mr. Charlie! You know, from the school lunchroom??

BO: Sure.

PHOEBE: Whatever.

LINDA: Sorry. Only trying to cheer everybody up.

BO: It didn't work.

LINDA: Look, we'll be fine. Pagasqueeny will leave soon, and we'll sneak out.

PAGASQUEENY: *Nothing* is where it should be.

>   (*He picks up the envelope of money, stares at it in confusion, tosses it into the trash. He then returns to preparing the food. He notices the pencils again.*)

PHOEBE: Dumb money. I should have just waited until Monday, when I come back to work. This is all your fault, Linda.

LINDA: You keep saying that.

PHOEBE: *You're* the one that spilled the pencils.

PAGASQUEENY: Stupid pencils all over the place.

PHOEBE: Didn't you do that at your last job too, Linda?

LINDA: Huh?

BO: Yeah! At that diner!

PHOEBE: Didn't you spill french fries all over the floor?

BO: And burn the hamburgers???

PHOEBE: Weren't you careless *there* too?

LINDA: What are you saying?

PHOEBE: Nothing.

LINDA: Yes, you are.

PHOEBE: I'm not saying anything.

BO: *I* am!

LINDA: I told you what happened. That diner closed! The Board of Health shut it down.

PHOEBE: It's awful interesting that the place where *you* worked was shut down by the Board of Health.

BO: Yep! Phoebe's got a point there.
    (Checking the peephole.)

LINDA: Okay. Wow. That's pretty low.

PHOEBE: Well . . .

LINDA: I mean, let's be honest here.

PHOEBE: Yeah, why don't we?

LINDA: You guys have been making those kinds of comments for a few weeks now. I know lately we've had a hard time getting along. But . . .

PHOEBE: Sorry. But I'm upset. And the truth, well . . . sometimes the truth hurts.

BO: Yep.

(Enter JESSIE and LUKE.)

LINDA: Well . . . you know, Phoebe, we aren't all lucky to have such a good job.

PHOEBE: Whatever.

BO: Wait, Phoebe. Who are those kids?

PHOEBE: What?

BO: Two kids just came into the kitchen.

(PHOEBE goes to the peephole to look.)

LUKE: Grandpa?

PAGASQUEENY: Yes??

JESSIE: Can you help us with the TV?

PHOEBE: Those are his grandkids!

PAGASQUEENY: I'm busy!

PHOEBE: What are they doing here??

LUKE: We want to watch 'Robots and Tacos'!

JESSIE: Yeah, it's our favorite cartoon!

PAGASQUEENY: But I'm making lunch!

LUKE: Grandpa, please!!

JESSIE: We can't find the right channel.

PAGASQUEENY: Oh, alright! Come on!

LUKE: Yay!

PAGASQUEENY: What show is it? *Robots and Tacos??*

LUKE: Yes!

JESSIE: It's the best show ever!

PAGASQUEENY: Lord . . . .

(They all exit.)

PHOEBE: Brats!

LINDA: Are they gone?

PHOEBE: Yes! Now look, here's what we'll do. Bo and I will go out the front door and then ring the doorbell. Then *you* sneak out the back while he's distracted.

LINDA: Why can't we all go out the front door?

PHOEBE: Too risky! You are clumsy! You'll make too much noise.

BO: Yeah!

PHOEBE: We'll go first! I'll pretend that I forgot my backpack and I came to get it. Linda, you sneak out the back door while he's distracted!

BO: Great idea!

PHOEBE: Okay, come on, Bo! Remember, Linda: we'll go out the front door. Then, we'll ring the doorbell and when he's distracted, you leave!

LINDA: Out the front door, right?

BO: No, *you* go out the back door!

LINDA: Oh! Where is that?

PHOEBE: It's in the back, you birdbrain!

LINDA: Oh, right!

(They exit hurriedly. Pause. LINDA comes out of the pantry, still confused. She begins to exit through the front door but then remembers and turns around to retreat to the back door. She knocks over an object from the table. Enter PAGASQUEENY.)

PAGASQUEENY: Uh . . . yes?? Can I help you?

LINDA: Oh, hello there! So sorry—I just—you know, I just came on in. Oh, I knocked over something here. *(Bends to pick it up.)*

PAGASQUEENY: You are the new worker from the referral service?

LINDA: Oh . . . oh, *yes*! Yes, I am. Sorry, I didn't knock. I just decided to come on in and get started!

PAGASQUEENY: Well, that's fine, I guess. I didn't expect you until tomorrow.

(The doorbell rings.)

LINDA: Oh, well, you know, I'm always early! No sir, I *hate* being late.

PAGASQUEENY: *(Notices the chef hat.)* I see. You came dressed for work. I like that.

LINDA: Oh, this old thing? Oh, well, you know, dress for success!

PAGASQUEENY: I see. Tell me about yourself.

LINDA: Well, I'm a … a worker. And a pretty good cook. And like I said, I'm always on time.

PAGASQUEENY: So you've said.

(The doorbell rings again.)

LINDA: Uh, aren't you going to get that?

PAGASQUEENY: No. It's probably just my idiot neighbor. He's always trying to borrow a cup of sugar or something.

LINDA: Oh. Okay.

PAGASQUEENY: Tell me, do you mind loud music in the house while you work?

LINDA: Oh, are you kidding me? I just love music of all kinds. Especially classical music! The timpani, and the trombones!

PAGASQUEENY: Splendid. Splendid.

LINDA: And you know, I—

PAGASQUEENY: What about making a mess? Do you make a mess when you work?

LINDA: Never! I'm the cleanest cook you'll lay eyes on. And you know what else I do?

PAGASQUEENY: What?

LINDA: I return things to where they *belong*. Everything has a place, right?

PAGASQUEENY: Everything. And never forget that!!

LINDA: Never!
  (Salutes him.)

PAGASQUEENY: Well. Good. There is one more thing. But first, what is your name?

LINDA: Linda.

PAGASQUEENY: Linda. Okay, there is one thing I've learned, Miss Linda.

LINDA: What is that?

PAGASQUEENY: Loyalty is hard to find.

LINDA: I know. I agree.

PAGASQUEENY: A good loyal worker, or a good loyal friend. They are extremely hard to find.

LINDA: Wow. I COMPLETELY agree.

PAGASQUEENY: So we'll see how you do. I didn't expect you until tomorrow, but I suppose we can get started. I was just making lunch. Can you make egg salad?

LINDA: Egg salad? It's my favorite!

PAGASQUEENY: Well, it's my least favorite.

LINDA: Oh.

(The doorbell rings again.)

PAGASQUEENY: But today I wanted it for some reason. Plus, my grandkids like it. Perhaps you can finish making it.

LINDA: Okay.

PAGASQUEENY: Isn't life strange? We don't eat certain things for a long time. And then out of nowhere we have the urge to eat them again.
(He laughs.)
Who knows what surprises each day will bring?

LINDA: You can say that again!

(Doorbell rings again. PAGASQUEENY begins to exit to the other part of the house.)

PAGASQUEENY: Okay, hop to it!

LINDA: Yes sir! Oh, uh, aren't you going to get that?

PAGASQUEENY: Oh, no. I told you. It's probably just my annoying neighbor. **(He says a well-known expression in Italian here.)**

LINDA: Uh . . . what does that mean?

PAGASQUEENY: Old Italian expression. In English it simply means 'no donkey-brains are welcome here.'

LINDA: Donkey-brains!! Okay!

PAGASQUEENY: Miss Linda . . .
(He presses play-button on the boombox. A classical piece begins to play)
I've got a good feeling about you.

*(He exits. LINDA, still surprised, begins to prepare the meal, waving her hands in time to the music. ** BO and PHOEBE may look through a window in shock, if this is possible ** End of play.)*

Four student monologues

☞

Ya'll is All

*A one-to-two minute monologue. Middle or high school. This is a humorous discussion of one of the other ways to say 'you guys' that many people seldom hear. There's **you guys,** there's **you all** . . . and then there's even one more! A funny but enlightening glance at the different ways that people communicate around the country.*

So . . . how come every time I say this word people look at me like I have two heads? Huh? Why is that? *Ya'll* is short for you guys. You people. You all. In Spanish, they say *ustedes.* Ya'll. Not a big deal, right? Or at least, it shouldn't be. Sure, I know. Usually people from the South are the ones that say it. But not always. Not always. A lot of people in other parts of the country say it. I hear it all the time. I also hear it on the television. From songs on the radio. *Ya'll coming to the birthday party? Ya'll gotta work on Thursday?* And so on . . .

So, you guys wanna try it? (*Motions to the audience to join him) Ya'll.* Right, just like that. Ya'll. Ready? One more time. One, two, three . . YA'LL. Good! That's it! What did you think? That wasn't so bad, was it?

Okay. Well, I gotta go, you guys. Oops! I gotta go, *ya'll!* Until next time . . .

The *Spanish* are Spanish

A one-minute monologue, specifically designed for a Latino student. Male or female.

Okay, I gotta get this out there. Ready? You sure? So check it out . . . we're not Spanish people. Got it? People from *Spain* are Spanish, and last time I checked there wasn't anybody in my school from Spain. I know, I know . . . there are plenty of Spaniards in the United States; but I meet a lot more Mexicans, Dominicans, Puerto Ricans, and even Ecuadorians in this country than I do Spaniards. A lot more. There *are* Spanish people in the United States, I get that. But unless you know that somebody is from Spain, you shouldn't call them Spanish. Spanish is what we *speak*. We're Hispanics. Latinos. Pick one. But not *Spanish people*!! Porque nosotros no somos de

España! Está bien? *(Pause.)* Whew! *(Wipes brow or forehead in relief)* Excellent. Thank you.

Yo Soy Salvadoreña

This three-to-four minute monologue is specifically written for a Latino student but any student of any gender can perform the monologue. The pauses are meant to suggest that the performer is waiting while somebody else speaks or asks him/her a particular question.

Hola. Cómo te va? Bien? Pues, yo estoy bien.

(Pause.)

What's that? Oh, sí. Yo soy Latina. That's right. Yo hablo español. And English too, of course. That's right. But before you ask . . . yo soy salvadoreña. I was born in the United States but my parents were born in El Salvador. So that makes me Salvadoran. Or at least, a Salvadoran-American. That's a tough one to say! I bet you thought I was Mexican, didn't you? You didn't? Okay. Well, that's fine if you did. You see, many people do. They look at me and they just assume that I'm Mexican. I mean, *all kinds of people* assume that! I get it almost every day. But it's okay. Well, at least sometimes it's okay. I have plenty of friends that are Mexican-Americans. Some of my neighbors are Mexican-Americans. They're Latinos, just like me. But although Mexico is only a few hundred miles from El Salvador, Mexicans aren't Salvadorans. You know? We still have our own culture and our own ways of doing things. For example, Salvadorans eat *pupusas*, not gorditas! What's a pupusa? It's kind of like a tortilla, stuffed with cheese, beans, and pork. The pupusa is strictly Salvadoran. Another thing is that some of us speak Caliche, which is a form of Spanish; but a lot of the words and phrases in caliche are different. Caliche is a Salvadoran thing. It's what many of us use. It's how we speak.

So, please: don't assume that all Latinos are Mexicans. It's better to just say *Latinos*. But if you *really* want to know our exact ancestry, just ask! *Con permiso. Yo estaba curioso . . .de dónde es tu familia?* "Excuse me – I was only curious. Where is your family from?" And I'll simply say . . . El Salvador! Just like that. Right?

(Pause. He or she can give a quick laugh here.)

Me llamo Isabel. I'm an American. I'm Latina. But I'm also Salvadoran!

(End.)

Dos, not *Do!*

A Duet

This three-to-four minute dual monologue is designed for one male and one female. The boy is to represent a Puerto Rican student, one who typically "eats their s's" when he/she speaks Spanish. The girl is Mexican-American, and her Spanish is slightly different than his. The two banter back and forth, in a competitive but friendly manner.

Any student of any race or gender can perform these roles.

GIRL: Hola. Qué tal?

BOY: Oye. Qué honda?

GIRL: Yo soy mexicana.

BOY: Yo sé. Yo soy boricua.

GIRL: You're what?

BOY: Boricua.

GIRL Oh. Yeah, I've heard of that. You're Hispanic.

BOY: Sí. Pero yo soy boricua también.

GIRL: I thought you were Puerto Rican!

BOY: I am! But sometimes we say *boricua*. It's the same thing, basically.

GIRL: Oh.

BOY: It demonstrates our pride, and the love of our culture.

GIRL: Oh. Okay. Yeah, you guys eat your s's.

BOY: Huh?

GIRL: Puerto Ricans eat their s's!

BOY: Oye, we speak Spanish the way we want to.

GIRL: Well, so do we. It's *cómo estás?*

BOY: It's como *está.*

GIRL: It is not.

BOY: It is too. How do you say the number 'two'?

GIRL: Two.

BOY: Huh?

GIRL: You said, 'how do you say two?' Well, it's *two!*

BOY: En español!

GIRL: Oh, right! Okay. Two is *dos*.

BOY: It's *do*.

GIRL: It's *dos*.

BOY: It's *do*. Tú está loca.

GIRL: It's *tú estás loca*! There you go! Eating your s's!

BOY: At least we don't say *pastel*.

GIRL: What?

BOY: Mexicans call cake 'pastel.'

GIRL: Well, what do you guys say?

BOY: Bizcocho!!

GIRL: Ahh, caramba!

BOY: And what about sports? All you guys talk about is soccer.

GIRL: Soccer rules!

BOY: No, *baseball* rules.

GIRL: Por favor. *(Sarcastically)* Baseball . . .

BOY: So . . . who is right? Puerto Ricans say bizcocho.

GIRL: Mexicans say pastel. We like soccer.

BOY: And we like baseball. I say *do*.

GIRL: And I say *dos*.

BOY: How do you say *tre*?

GIRL: *Tres*!!

BOY: Ahh! Of course.

GIRL: So . . . who is right?

BOY: Well, the answer is . . .

BOY & GIRL: We're both right!

BOY: I say things my way.

GIRL: And I say things my way.

BOY: There's more than one way to experience Latino culture.

GIRL: And there's more than one way to speak Spanish. *(Quietly.)* Even though it's *dos*, not *do*.

BOY: Oye! I heard that.

GIRL: Discúlpame.

BOY: Hmmph.

(They both face the front, boldly and proudly.)

GIRL: Yo soy mexicana.

BOY: Y yo soy boricua. Nosotros somos Latinos.

GIRL: Y también somos americanos.

BOY: We both speak Spanish.

GIRL: We just speak it in different ways.

(End.)

Monologues are free. But please consult us before using in a competition or performance. **john@studentplays.org**

☞ **More from Student Plays** ☜

Othello's Just Another Fellow

Dramedy. Middle School/upper Elementary. 25-35 minutes. 6 actors: 3 males, 3 females, one teacher (or student portraying a teacher) 4 to 6 extra actors, if needed. ****A Latino-themed play****

A group of students are involved in a school production of *Othello*, but one of them is disturbed about the lack of diversity in the play. He takes certain steps to disrupt the play but in the end is encouraged by the others to try and make a difference in another, more constructive way. A lesson is learned, and the production is saved from disaster!

Pagasqueeny's Pantry

Comedy. **Middle/High School.** 15-20 minutes. 6 actors: 3 females, 2 males. One student (or a teacher) plays the comical role of the elderly Mr. Pagasqueeny.

Three friends sneak into Mr. Pagasqueeny's home to get something that one of them left behind. But in walks Pagasqueeny and they must hide in the pantry! In this comical play, a lesson is learned about honesty and trust, but it takes a heated discussion in the pantry and a subsequent attempt to escape to find this out!

Una Carta de Abuelo

Dramedy. Middle/High School. 35-45 minutes. 10 actors: 1 teacher, 5 females, 4 males. (With the possibility of 4-5 extra actors in two classroom scenes.)   **A Latino-themed play**

Two cousins discover an old letter in their late grandfather's comic collection that they think leads to treasure! The cousins often butt heads, with one believing that he is more "Mexican," the other believing that some people make too much of a fuss about "being Mexican." Thus, they form their *own* groups in search of what Grandpa hid long ago. But what they find is actually worth more than merely silver or gold.

Barbecue at the Prom!

Dramedy. **Middle School/upper elementary.** 25-35 minutes. 6 actors: 3 females, 3 males

It's a classic tale of guys versus girls! It's a prom committee, and everybody is supposed to work together but differences and opinions get in the way, causing the guys and girls to form their groups. For the end-of-the-year prom, one side wants pasta and lace, the other wants sports and barbecue! The two groups square off but eventually work together, demonstrating the importance of cooperation and compromise.

Going to Guatemala

Dramedy. High School. 50-60 minutes. 11 actors. 6 males, 5 females.   ****A Latino-themed play****

A Latino student is chosen at the last minute to join a humanitarian group from his school that is headed to Guatemala. But since his Spanish is weak, he faces ridicule and criticism from certain peers. Jealousy and anger trickle throughout the campus as the trip approaches, and the social atmosphere of the high school becomes even more hectic when the student's trip money is stolen on campus, jeopardizing his trip.

Stravinsky's Kitchen

Comedy. **High School/College.** 12-15 minutes. 3 actors: 3 males (or females).

Two friends secretly enter the home of an employer to obtain a forgotten object but the homeowner abruptly arrives home while they are there. As they hide in the kitchen's pantry and plot their getaway, the two talk and eventually argue, exposing the true colors of one of them. Upon their hasty exit a mistake is made, and one of them capitalizes on this mistake, resulting in his/her fortune.

Forty Whacks

Drama. Spooky. **High School/College.** 25-35 minutes. 3 actors: 2 females, 1 male.

A pair of siblings have inherited the Lizzie Borden Bed and Breakfast in New England. Although the business was run for decades in a quiet, respectable fashion, one of the siblings is over-ambitious, wanting to unearth an alleged piece of buried evidence within the house. This brings about a chilly tension between brother and sister, and perhaps within the house itself.

John Calhoun and a Thief

Drama. **College.** 35-40 minutes. 3 actors: 2 females, 1 male.

Kicked out of a university PhD program, a bitter and dejected female lifts from the library archives original copies of John Calhoun's personal documents. Counseled and consoled by her roommates, her conscience slowly gets to her; but as she seeks entry to other universities her luck turns to worse, and the subsequent decisions she makes regarding the historic papers cause this one-act play to become darker, if not funnier.

Honoring the Hijacker

Drama. **College.** 12-15 minutes. 4 actors: 2 females, 2 males.

It's 1981, the ten-year anniversary of the famed hijacker D.B. Cooper. The play's four characters are attending a "D.B. Festival" and have stayed up very late, outlasting everybody else. The late night chit-chat goes from pranks and jokes to outright volatility, and suddenly this get-together becomes something that three of the four characters didn't bargain for.

It's a Super Day at Sammy's!

Comedy. **Middle or High School.** 35-40 minutes. 9 actors: 5 females, 4 males (4 possible adults).

Jodi has found a summer job at a travel agency. But her three younger siblings can't seem to live without her! They call her at the office incessantly, which interferes with the work. The standard telephone greeting "It's a super day at Sammy's!" becomes a repeated theme of this comedy, as Jodi struggles to reach a balance between her job and her nagging siblings

Three Tenners

Comedy/Drama. **Elementary through High School.** Three Ten-Minute Plays.

Three Creepy Plays

Drama. **Middle School through College.** Three short 'creepy' plays.

Hockey Masks in Hueytown

Drama. Spooky. **High School/College.** 20-25 minutes. 4 actors: 2 males, 2 females.

Driving home for Thanksgiving break, four college students stop off in a small rural town to retrieve one of the student's old family pictures. They reluctantly enter the empty home of his deceased uncle, a former producer for the Friday the 13th movies. Strange objects are found during their search . . but when a hockey mask surfaces, everything really goes sideways.

The Witch Makes Five

Drama. Spooky. **High School.** 10 minutes. 4 actors: 2 males, 2 females.

After a bizarre group camping trip, a student is checked into a youth mental facility . When she is visited by the other members of the trip, memories of the weekend trickle out . . . and horrific things begin to happen.

Mrs. Calapooza and the Culebra

Dramedy. **Grades 5-8.** 10 minutes. 5 actors: 3 females, 2 males.

Fed up with their grouchy teacher's classroom ways, four students complain and bicker back and forth during a Spanish quiz. The situation grows worse when the friends discover that one of them has pulled the ultimate prank on the teacher.

Raiders of the Lost Rakasa

Dramedy. **Grades 5-8.** 10 minutes. 7 actors: 4 females, 3 males.

Seven young explorers arrive at a cave in a far-off land in search of the great "Rakasa." They find what they want . . . along with a few of the cave's unexpected surprises.